ATLAS OF COUNTRIES

Created by Gallimard Jeunesse,
Claude Delafosse, and Donald Grant
Illustrated by Donald Grant

A FIRST DISCOVERY BOOK

Note: Atlas of Countries is a child's very first atlas.
Using simplified maps, bright illustrations, and basic
information, it introduces young children to the
diversity of countries all over the world.

O7-CQS-317

Cartwheel
·B·O·O·K·S· ®
SCHOLASTIC INC.
New York   Toronto   London   Auckland   Sydney

A globe is a
three-dimensional map
of the earth. When it is rotated,
the globe shows different halves,
called hemispheres, of the earth.
Turn the globe
to see the other hemisphere.

Maps drawn on paper show
land areas, oceans, and seas, too.
But unlike the globe, a flat map can
show two hemispheres at once.

On the globe, the earth looks perfectly round.
But did you know that the earth is
slightly flat at the North and South poles?

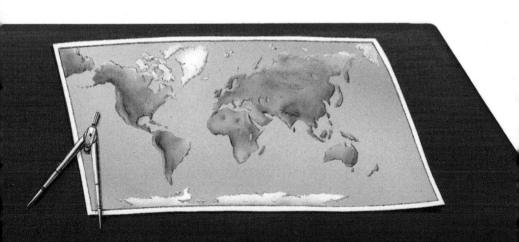

The earth is constantly moving. Every 24 hours, it spins once around its axis, an imaginary line that runs between the North and South poles. As the earth spins (rotates), it also travels (revolves) around the sun. It takes the earth one year to travel completely around the sun.

The rotation of the earth causes night and day.
The part of the earth facing the sun has daylight.
The side turned away from the sun
does not get sunlight and so has night.

Scientists believe the earth was formed 4½ billion years ago.

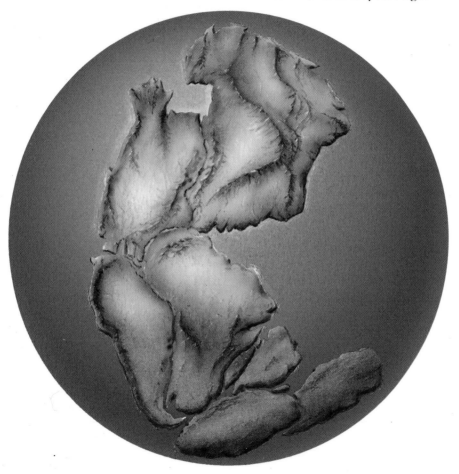

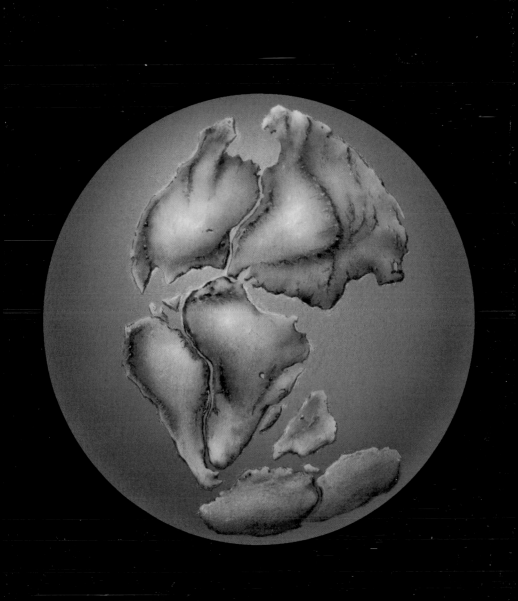

Scientists think that the earth once had
one huge land mass.
Then about 200 million years ago,
it began to divide into several parts.

The parts slowly moved away from one another.
The largest parts became the continents we have today.

The continents make up only about 30 percent of the earth's surface. The rest is water. Turn the page to compare the surface of water covering the globe to that of the land forming the continents.

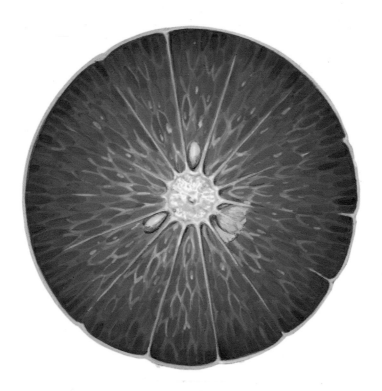

This orange represents the earth.
The thick outer skin of the earth is its crust.
Underneath the crust is the mantle and the outer core.
The inner core is at the very center.

Most of the water found on earth is in the oceans. Oceans and other bodies of water, ice, and water vapor in the air make up the earth's hydrosphere.

The waters of the hydrosphere are very important. People, animals, and plants need water to live.

Now, let's look at each continent, starting at the poles.

Here is the Arctic.
At its center is the North Pole
surrounded by the Arctic Ocean.

The climate is almost always cold.
But in summer, there is no snow
and ice in most of the Arctic.

Here is the Antarctic.
Located at the South Pole, it is the
coldest continent on Earth.

There are no people here, except
for the scientists and explorers who
travel to Antarctica to study.

These capital letters represent countries in Europe.
Use the letters to find these countries on the map.

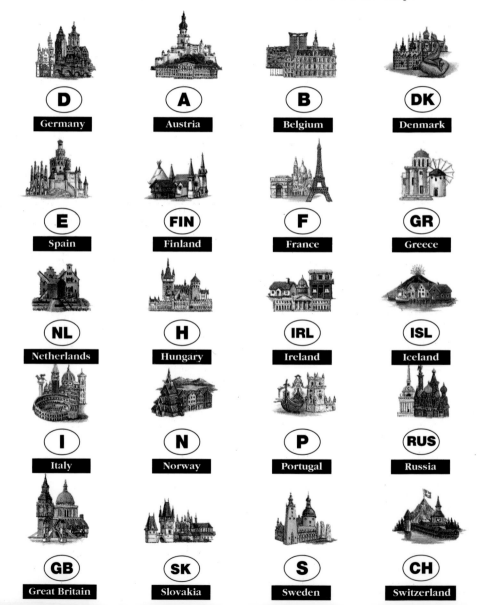

D Germany

A Austria

B Belgium

DK Denmark

E Spain

FIN Finland

F France

GR Greece

NL Netherlands

H Hungary

IRL Ireland

ISL Iceland

I Italy

N Norway

P Portugal

RUS Russia

GB Great Britain

SK Slovakia

S Sweden

CH Switzerland

Russia is the biggest country in Europe.

ISL Iceland

Norwegian Sea

Sweden

FIN Finland

Norway

N

S

Baltic Sea

Estonia

Latvia

RUS Russia

North Sea

Lithuania

Ireland

IRL Great Britain

DK Denmark

Belarus

GB Netherlands

Poland

NL Germany

Ukraine

Belgium

B

D

Czech Republic

Atlantic Ocean

Luxembourg

Slovakia

SK

Moldova

Austria

F

A

H Hungary

France

CH

Slovenia

Romania

Switzerland

Croatia

Yugoslavia

Black Sea

Portugal

Bosnia and Herzegovina

Bulgaria

P

I

E

Italy

Albania

Turkey

Spain

GR Greece

Mediterranean Sea

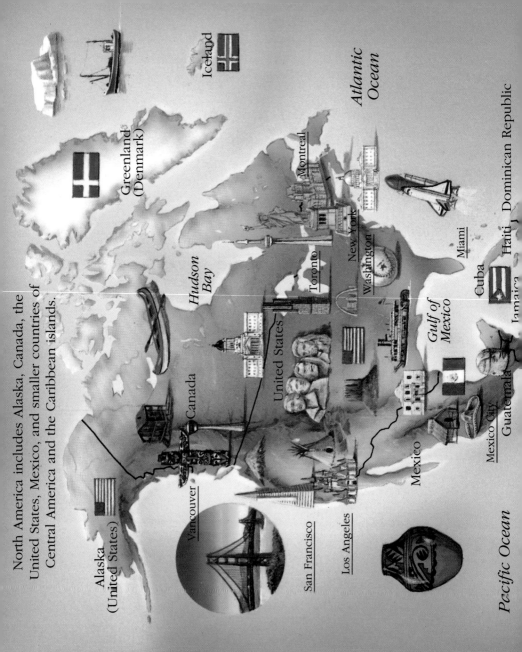

North America includes Alaska, Canada, the United States, Mexico, and smaller countries of Central America and the Caribbean islands.

Iceland

Atlantic Ocean

Greenland (Denmark)

Montreal

New York

Miami

Dominican Republic

Haiti

Cuba

Jamaica

Hudson Bay

Toronto

Washington

Gulf of Mexico

United States

Canada

Mexico

Mexico City

Guatemala

Vancouver

Alaska (United States)

San Francisco

Los Angeles

Pacific Ocean

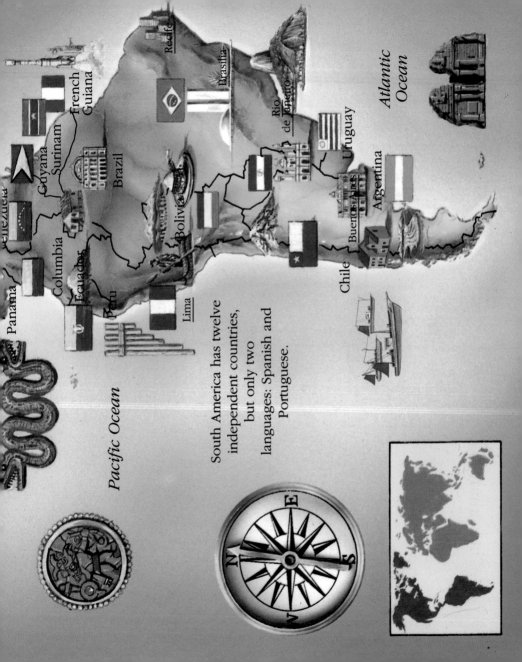

Panama

VENEZUELA

French Guiana

Guyana

Surinam

Columbia

Brazil

Ecuador

Peru

Bolivia

Lima

Recife

Brasília

Rio de Janeiro

Uruguay

Argentina

Buenos Aires

Chile

Atlantic Ocean

Pacific Ocean

South America has twelve independent countries, but only two languages: Spanish and Portuguese.

N E S W

Africa is the hottest continent.
The Sahara, the world's largest desert, is in the north.

Mediterranean
Sea

Red Sea

Algiers

Rabat

Morocco

Western
Sahara

Mauritania

Tunis
Tunisia

Tripoli

Libya

Algeria

Mali

Niger

Burkina
Faso

Cairo

Egypt

Sudan

Chad

Nigeria

Central
African
Republic

Cameroon

Djibouti

Somalia

Ethiopia

Senegal
Gambia
Guinea-Bissau
Guinea

Sierra Leone

Liberia

Côte
d'Ivoire

Ghana
Togo
Benin

Indian Ocean

Kenya
Nairobi
Uganda
Rwanda
Burundi
Zaire
Gabon
Congo
Tanzania
Malawi
Mozambique
Madagascar
Zimbabwe
Zambia
Angola
Namibia
Botswana
South Africa
Pretoria
Swaziland
Lesotho

Atlantic Ocean

Much of the African landscape is grassland. Thick tropical rain forests are found in central and western Africa.

Arctic Ocean

Western Siberian Plain

Russia (Russian Federation)

Kazakhstan

Uzbekistan

Georgia
Azerbaijan
Turkey
Armenia
Turkmenistan
Kyrgyzstan

Tajikistan

Lebanon Syria
Israel
Jordan
Iraq
Kuwait
Iran
Afghanistan

Pakistan

Tibetan Plateau

Nepal

Saudi Arabia
Qatar
United Arab Emirates
Oman
Yemen

India

The climate in Asia varies from the cold polar regions to the hot tropical south.

Sri Lanka

Indian Ocean

Asia is the largest continent, and it also has the most people.

Mongolia

Japan

North Korea

Beijing

South Korea

China

Tokyo

Bangladesh

Taiwan

Pacific Ocean

anmar

umar Laos

Hong Kong

Thailand

Phillipines

angkok Cambodia

Vietnam

Malaysia

Singapore

New Guinea

Indonesia

People have found a handy way to locate countries
and other features on a map. Their positions are set within lines
of longitude and latitude. Lines of latitude, like the equator,
circle the globe. Lines of longitude run parallel to the
prime meridian. All of these lines are numbered in degrees.

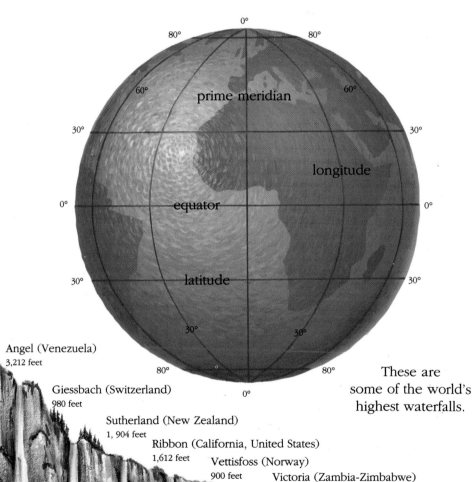

These are
some of the world's
highest waterfalls.

Angel (Venezuela)
3,212 feet

Giessbach (Switzerland)
980 feet

Sutherland (New Zealand)
1, 904 feet

Ribbon (California, United States)
1,612 feet

Vettisfoss (Norway)
900 feet

Victoria (Zambia-Zimbabwe)
355 feet

Niagara
(United States-Canada)
176 feet

At any given moment, the hour in many parts of the world is different.
That's because the world is divided into 24 time zones.
Each time zone is one hour ahead or
one hour behind the zone on either side.
In this picture, the earth is divided into twelve sections.
Each section represents two time zones.

Here are
some of the world's
highest mountains.

Mt. Everest
(Nepal)
29,028 feet

Aconcagua
(Argentina)
22,831 feet

Mt. McKinley
(Alaska,
United States)
20,320 feet

Kilimanjaro
(Tanzania)
19,340 feet

Mt. Blanc
(France)
15,771 feet

Matterhorn
(Switzerland)
14,692 feet

Mt. Fuji
(Japan)
12,388 feet

Mt. Cook
(New Zealand)
12,349 feet

Titles in the series of *First Discovery Books:*

**Airplanes
and Flying Machines
All About Time
Bears
*Birds
*Boats
*The Camera
Cars and Trucks
and Other Vehicles
*Castles
Cats
Colors
Dinosaurs
The Earth and Sky
The Egg

**Flowers
Fruit
The Ladybug and
Other Insects
Light
Musical Instruments
Pyramids
The Rain Forest
*The River
The Seashore
**The Tree
Under the Ground
Vegetables in the
Garden
Water
***Weather
*Whales**

Titles in the series of
*First Discovery
Art* Books:

**Animals
Landscapes
Paintings
Portraits**

Titles in the series of
*First Discovery
Atlas* Books:

**Atlas of Animals
Atlas of Countries
Atlas of People
Atlas of Plants**

*Parents Magazine
"Best Books" Award

**Parenting Magazine
Reading Magic Award

***Oppenheim Toy Portfolio
Gold Seal Award

Library of Congress Cataloging-in-Publication Data available.

Originally published in France under the title *Atlas des pays* by Editions Gallimard.

ISBN 0-590-58282-8

12 11 10 9 8 7 6 5 4 3 2 1   6 7 8 9/9 0 1/0
Printed in Italy by Editoriale Libraria
First Scholastic printing, March 1996